LEGENDS OF WARFARE

GROUND

Tigers I and II

Germany's Most Feared Tanks of World War II

DAVID DOYLE

SCHIFFER MILITARY

4880 Lower Valley Road   Atglen, PA 19310

Designed by Justin Watkinson
Type set in Impact/Minion Pro/Univers LT Std

ISBN: 978-0-7643-5848-7
Printed in China

Published by Schiffer Publishing, Ltd.
4880 Lower Valley Road
Atglen, PA 19310
Phone: (610) 593-1777; Fax: (610) 593-2002
E-mail: Info@schifferbooks.com
www.schifferbooks.com

For our complete selection of fine books on this and related subjects, please visit our website at www.schifferbooks.com. You may also write for a free catalog.

Schiffer Publishing's titles are available at special discounts for bulk purchases for sales promotions or premiums. Special editions, including personalized covers, corporate imprints, and excerpts, can be created in large quantities for special needs. For more information, contact the publisher.

We are always looking for people to write books on new and related subjects. If you have an idea for a book, please contact us at proposals@schifferbooks.com.

Acknowledgments

This book would not have been possible without the gracious help of many individuals and institutions. Beyond the invaluable help provided by the staffs of the Bundesarchiv, the National Archives, and the Patton Museum, I am deeply indebted to Massimo Foti, John Blackman, Pat Stansell, Scott Taylor, and Don Moriarty. Their generous and skillful assistance adds immensely to the quality of this volume. In addition to such wonderful friends and colleagues, the Lord has blessed me with a wonderful wife, Denise, who has tirelessly scanned thousands of photos and documents for this and numerous other books. Beyond that, she is an ongoing source of support and inspiration. The front cover photo is courtesy of John Blackman.

Contents

Introduction		004
CHAPTER 1	**Tiger I**	006
CHAPTER 2	**Tiger II**	076

Introduction

Both Henschel and Porsche competed for the July 1941 *Wehrmacht* requirement for a new heavy tank. Both prototypes were known as VK 45.01, but the Porsche version is known as the VK 45.01 (P) and is sometimes referred to as the Tiger (P). It used a turret designed by Krupp that mounted the potent 8.8 cm KwK L/56 high-velocity gun. The unique drivetrain design used two V-10 air-cooled engines that drove generators to power the front sprockets. The power system was similar to that used on railroad Diesel-electric locomotives and eliminated the need for a transmission. Technicians confer on the rear deck of this VK 45.01 (P) during tests at Döllersheim. *The Tank Museum*

The Tiger was Germany's most feared tank of World War II. Both the Tiger I and the later Tiger *Ausführung* (Model) *B* (*Ausf. B*) or Tiger II, were formidable fighting machines, and the German propaganda ministry made sure to amplify the Tiger's effectiveness, while masking its numerous deficiencies. Among the latter were complexity, cost, and reliability. These problems had plagued the Tiger from day one—and abated but a little as the design evolved.

In 1937, in response to a request from the German military, Daimler-Benz, Henschel, and M.A.N. all presented heavy-tank designs. In 1939, Porsche too became involved. While the Daimler and M.A.N. designs ultimately evolved into the Panther, the Porsche and Henschel designs formed the basis for the Tiger.

As originally presented by Henschel, the main gun of the new tank would be a tapered-bore weapon, starting at 7.5 cm and exiting the muzzle at 5 cm. While the pressures developed in a tapered-bore design imparted great muzzle velocity, Germany's acute shortage of tungsten, essential to making the rounds, precluded its use.

From Dr. Ferdinand Porsche's camp came the opinion that the standard mechanical power train was too weak to bear the high loads imposed by a heavy tank. Accordingly, his 88 mm-armed offering, the Typ 100, also known as the VK 3001 (P), provided for the use of a gas-electric drivetrain.

Two large V-10 gasoline engines would turn generators, which in turn would supply the current to a pair of electric motors that would act as final drives. While ultimately Porsche's firm would receive an order for one wooden mockup and three trial vehicles, ultimately only the mockup and a single unarmed pilot was produced.

In May 1941, Adolf Hitler ordered that frontal armor of the proposed new heavy tank be increased to 100 mm. Initially the redesigned heavy tank received the army designation VK 4501 (P), while the Porsche company called it Typ 101, but in June, the vehicle was redesignated *Panzerkampfwagen VI Tiger*. A pair of 15-liter engines powered the generators.

The turret design of the VK3001, which originated from Krupp, who also served the Henschel heavy-tank design, was retained. By August 1941, the heavy-tank project was known as the *Tigerprogramm*, and a push was underway to complete a prototype, followed by an initial order of 100 tanks.

A trial vehicle was sent to Hitler's Rastenburg headquarters in East Prussia for a competition with the Henschel vehicle—on the occasion of Hitler's birthday, April 20, 1942. Although the Porsche design was initially favored, its performance was lackluster, frequently becoming mired and breaking down and its engines consuming excessive oil. Ultimately, the 100 tanks of the initial order would be the sole order, and most of those were completed as *Jagdpanzers* (self-propelled antitank guns) rather than tanks. In fact, only a single example of this type would see combat, being deployed in April 1944 and knocked out in July.

So confident was Porsche in its design that they began limited production of the vehicle. The testing seen here was done in the hope that the tanks could equip the *schwere Panzerabteilung 501* in Tunisia. However, fine-tuning the design was to last much longer than anticipated. Most of the vehicles were later converted into *Ferdinand* and then *Elefant* tank destroyers, as well as a few tank recovery units. *Patton Museum*

A single VK 45.01 (P) was used in combat by the *Panzerjäger Abteilung 653*, a unit on the Eastern Front deploying *Ferdinand/Elefant* tank destroyers. The vehicle was the final one completed by the manufacturer, Nibelungenwerk, in the fall of 1942. It was chassis number 150013 and was built as a *Befehlswagen*. Although it had been retained at the factory for testing, it was eventually modified in a manner similar to the tank destroyers. It became the mount of *Hauptmann* Grillenberg from April to July 1944, when it was lost in combat. *Tom Laemlein collection*

With the decision made to further develop the Henschel design, work began in earnest. Owing to the mandated weight increase, the result of increasing armor and larger armament, wider tracks were required in order to lower ground pressure. Accordingly, the track width was increased from 520 mm to 725 mm. This required an additional roadwheel arrangement to be added to the design. Located outboard of the two rows of initially planned roadwheel stations, the additional roadwheel required wider tracks. These then would make the Tiger too wide for rail transport. To overcome this, a second set of tracks, known as *Verladeketten* ("transportation tracks") and being only 520 mm wide, were developed for use during railroad transport.

To install the *Verladeketten*, the operational *Marschketten* or "combat tracks" along with the outer roadwheels had to be removed. Upon arrival at a destination, and before going into the field, the process was reversed, a labor-intensive task that an experienced tank crew could accomplish in about thirty minutes.

This is just one of the logistical problems brought about by fielding this vehicle. Though a massive, well-armed, and well-protected combat vehicle, the Tiger was a burden on the German manufacturing base; it was plagued by automotive and maintenance deficiencies and was extremely costly, with a unit price about four times that of a *Sturmgeschütz*.

Power for the Tiger came from Maybach engines. The first 250 Tigers were powered by a 21-liter, 650-horsepower HL210 P30. Subsequently, the 23-liter Maybach HL230 P45 engine, developing 700 horsepower, was installed instead. After 391 Tigers had been built, a new commander's cupola based on that of the Panther was introduced, as was a turret escape hatch. A better cupola mount for the MG 34 began to be used in July 1943, and two months later the number of headlights on Tiger tanks was reduced to only one.

The suspension on the Tiger tanks was of torsion-bar type, and after approximately 800 tanks had been manufactured, in January 1944 the factory switched from the previously used rubber-tired roadwheels to what were called "steel road wheels." Based on a Soviet design, the latter conserved precious rubber and, due to their increased load capacity, allowed for fewer roadwheels per vehicle to be installed.

While initially known as the "Mark VI tank," on February 27, 1944, Hitler decreed that thereafter it would be referred to as "Tiger Tank *Ausführung E*" (*Ausf. E*). The last of the Tiger I *Ausf. E*s rolled out of the factory in August 1944. That vehicle—indeed, the last fifty-four Tiger Is—were interesting vehicles. Most were constructed using hulls of irreparably damaged Tigers salvaged from battlefields. Twenty-two of these required newly manufactured turrets.

During the two years of production spanning August 1942 through August 1944, 1,355 of the vehicles were built.

Although powerfully armed and boasting heavy armor, the substantial weight of the Tiger I—56 tons—pushed suspension and power-train components to their limits. With Germany chronically short on gasoline, the Tiger's mileage of less than 1 mile per gallon was a logistical hurdle as well. Ultimately, it is likely that a high percentage of the Tigers were deliberately destroyed by German troops after either running out of gas or suffering a breakdown.

Allied tanks could tackle the Tiger, and late in the war this could be done one on one on equal footing, but midwar victories required skill and cunning to make up for the disparity in equipment.

The original Fgst.Nr. V1 Tiger I. This vehicle was completed in April 1942, and this photo clearly shows the *Vorpanzer* folding skirt stowed on the top of the front hull. This could be lowered down in front of the tank to protect the tracks. This was consistent with its design as a breakthrough tank. *The Tank Museum*

A closer view of the *Vorpanzer*. Although sound in concept, the device may have had limited utility in actual use. It contained no dampening mechanisms and was meant to be manually actuated. Additionally, there were no hooks or openings for the crew to lift it off or back on the hull. Perhaps its most critical deficiency was the solid armor plate located over the final drives (and under the shield). Even a small object could get jammed between it and the tracks, rendering the vehicle immovable. *The Tank Museum*

The very first production Tiger Is can be readily identified by the distinctive curved notches in the forward part of the front tow shackles. The notches were cut to accommodate part of the *Vorpanzer* mechanism when the shield was in its folded position. These very early tanks also did not have bolts for the side fenders. This vehicle is a battle-scarred veteran of the *schwere Panzerabteilung 502* and was photographed in the early summer of 1943. This tank was among the very first delivered to the unit at the end of 1942. *Patton Museum*

Among the first units to receive the Tiger I was the *schwere Panzerabteilung 501*. These tanks were initially shipped to Sicily, then transported to Tunisia by ferry in November 1942. Given this delivery date, all the tanks were early production vehicles. This vehicle mounts a full set of the *Feifel* air cleaner canisters. Many of the unique features of the 1st Company's vehicles can also be seen here, such as the fender flaps attached to the rear fenders, spare track mounts, and sheet-metal muffler covers. *Bundesarchiv*

Another prominent modification made by the *schwere Panzerabteilung 501* was the headlights mounted on angled bases, which were in turn mounted on the glacis plate. This tank still retains the notches for the *Vorpanzer* at the top of the tow shackle bases, making it a vehicle produced in late-summer 1942. The addition of side skirts was a unit modification. Note that they are not installed along a straight line. *Bundesarchiv*

An *SdKfz. 9* FAMO recovery half-track, along with what appears to be an *SdKfz. 7*, assist in the recovery of a Tiger I assigned to the 8th Company of *Panzer Regiment 7* in Tunisia. This tank still retains many of the modifications it received upon arrival in the theater, when it was assigned to the *schwere Panzer Abteilung 501*. The *Feifel* system has sustained severe damage and has been disconnected. A captured US Jeep is seen at the extreme right. *Patton Museum*

A captured US M2 half-track and 1-ton trailer follow a German Tiger I tank of *schwere Panzer Abteilung 501* in Tunisia in 1943. The trailer is carrying spare Tiger bogie wheels appropriately marked with the number "501." Since *schwere Panzerabteilung 504* was also active in the area at the time, scarce parts were cautiously guarded. *Bundesarchiv*

During a road march in Tunisia, an *SdKfz 251/7* half-track follows a Tiger I. Another modification characteristic of the Tigers of *schwere Panzer Abteilung 501* was the addition of twin brackets to support a track toolbox on the rear hull. This can be seen on the lower left side. Also noticeable are the *Feifel* air prefilters—still largely intact at this point. *Bundesarchiv*

In February 1943, *schwere Panzer Abteilung 501* was integrated into the *10th Panzer Division*, becoming the 7th and 8th Companies of its *Panzer Regiment 7*. Just prior to the integration, many of the tanks were repainted in order to make them blend better with the Tunisian terrain (with captured stocks of US Olive Drab, according to one source). When the Tigers were renumbered, their tactical numbers became red with a white outline. The tank shown here was originally vehicle number "132" when serving with the 1st Company of the *501*. *Bundesarchiv*

Strict instructions were laid down regarding Tigers falling into enemy hands. An elaborate and thorough demolition procedure was to be initiated in the event a vehicle could not be recovered. These two Tigers, tactical numbers "823" and "833," of the 8th Company, *7th Panzer Regiment*, were demolished according to these guidelines after the tanks were disabled near Bâjah (Béja), Tunisia. *Patton Museum*

On the hunt for souvenirs, GIs pick through the wreckage of two Tigers destroyed near Bâjah, Tunisia, during Operation *Ochsenkopf*. The vertical slats on each side of the glacis plate were put in place to hold three links of spare track—a modification characteristic of the 2nd Company of the *schwere Panzerabteilung 501*. Also note that the headlights remain mounted to the upper hull. *Tom Laemlein collection*

Tiger "323" of the *schwere Panzerabteilung 503* is a tank produced in December 1942 or January 1943 with a unique unit-made turret *Gepäckkasten*, since the date of manufacture predates the introduction of the stowage box. The relative thickness of the track cable can be seen here. The outside roadwheels have received several shrapnel hits. This Tiger also has the very early-style, flat tow shackles.
Patton Museum

Tiger number "123" of *schwere Panzer Abteilung 503* is seen in January 1943, just days after its arrival in Soviet territory. Its date of manufacture is probably November–December 1942. It mounts a modified *Panzer III* stowage bin on the rear of the turret, a temporary measure instituted at the factory during this time. The tank still retains the apertures for the KFF 2 driver's periscopes, eliminated in February 1943 production. *Patton Museum*

Another Tiger I of the *schwere Panzer Abteilung 503* is seen later that same month while undergoing maintenance. The late 1942 production features are somewhat clearer here: the driver's periscope apertures and the *Panzer III* type stowage bin. The latter item has been installed on metal stock extensions that space it away from the turret in order to permit access to the center-lifting pin located directly in front of the bin. The utility of this feature is being clearly demonstrated here. *Patton Museum*

A Tiger I approaches a boggy area. In spite of the width of its tracks, crews were strictly cautioned about traversing soft ground. The considerable weight of the tank would cause it to mire quite quickly, and for that same reason recovery could be difficult and time consuming. This tank still has the apertures above the driver's visor for the KFF 2 periscope, indicating production prior to February 1943. *National Archives*

Tiger I, tactical number "131" of *schwere Panzer Abteilung 504* as seen after its capture by the British. All of the unit's tanks were brand new when the 1st Company departed for Tunisia in March 1943. There are numerous perforations from projectiles on the muffler heat shields, turret stowage box, and air prefilters. The arm for the starter crank is installed on its shaft. This was normally stowed either on the top hull or in the turret stowage box.
The Tank Museum

British soldiers take a closer look at the engine compartment of number "131." It was captured after an engagement with a Churchill tank where a six-pounder round disabled its gun mount and turret. This Tiger, chassis number 250112 from February 1943 production, is now part of the collection at the Tank Museum, Bovington, and has been restored to running condition. *Patton Museum*

The 2nd Company of *schwere Panzer Abteilung 504* was deployed to Sicily in 1943 in support of the *Fallschirm-Panzer Division Herman Göring*. One of its Tigers sits abandoned there in July 1943. Only one of the battalion's seventeen Tigers survived to be evacuated to the Italian mainland. Like those of the 1st Company, this one appears to be February 1943 production. *Tom Laemlein collection*

A US DUKW amphibious truck squeezes past another abandoned Tiger I of 2nd Company, *schwere Panzer Abteilung 504*, in Sicily in July 1943. The single-chamber *Feifel* air canisters (installed in March) illustrate that this was a nearly brand-new machine when it arrived there in May. Another relatively new feature is the manual starter crank arm stowed on the lower right of the rear hull. This was added in February 1943 production. *Tom Laemlein collection*

This Tiger I, tactical number "100," shows no evidence at this angle of unit insignia. It features a camouflage scheme that is somewhat more elaborate than usual. Considerable effort has been applied to create an intricate disruptive pattern over the entire surface of the hull, including the *Feifel* air canisters and the rear exhaust shields. The *Feifel* air canisters are the later one-piece type, indicating production after March 1943. *Patton Museum*

A group of civilians prepare for their portraits on the top of a Tiger I. Although many of the fittings are hidden from view, several features can be seen to aid in identifying its production date. The welded periscope apertures above the driver's visor and the presence of the large shovel both indicate February 1943 production. *National Archives*

Two Tigers and a *Panzerkampfwagen III* are seen at a maintenance yard. A Fries Gantry Portalkran is in the background. The track toolbox frame and clasps for the starter crankshaft indicate production after February 1943. Although the muffler shields are removed, the small bolts that they were attached to remain. The lugs used to lift the armored guards for the exhaust bases are visible here as well. *National Archives*

Tiger crewmen of the *schwere Panzer Abteilung 502* clean the barrel of the 88 mm KwK 36 L/56 cannon while training at the old French artillery firing range of Coëtquidan, near Augan, Brittany. The chassis number can be seen next to the driver's armored visor. This indicates that the tank was one of fifty Tiger I tanks completed in April 1943. These numbers were typically painted over after unit delivery.
Patton Museum

The following are part of a series of photos shot in Shop 3 at Henschel's Mittelfeld Werkes plant during the construction of Tiger I hulls in the spring of 1943. Here, a turret ring is being precision milled by means of large jig. The last three digits of the chassis number are marked on the hull in chalk. *Patton Museum*

Here, several large, horizontal-spindle borers are cutting openings for the suspension components. The hulls were moved to these stands via a substantial system of lifting cranes that ran along the roof of the facility. *Patton Museum*

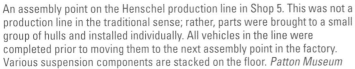

An assembly point on the Henschel production line in Shop 5. This was not a production line in the traditional sense; rather, parts were brought to a small group of hulls and installed individually. All vehicles in the line were completed prior to moving them to the next assembly point in the factory. Various suspension components are stacked on the floor. *Patton Museum*

Component installation continues in Shop 5, with an overhead crane lowering a Maybach engine into the hull. Other workers are installing bogie arms onto the torsion bars. There were eight bars and arms on each side. On the right the arms trailed to the rear, while on the left the arms faced the opposite direction. *Patton Museum*

Workers continue to guide the Maybach HL 245 engine into the tight confines of the engine compartment. A series of square bolts have been welded to the hull sides for later installation of fender panels. They will remain off the vehicle until after delivery. The addition of roadwheels has begun. The hull is raised off the surface of the factory floor in order to accommodate this. *Patton Museum*

The HL210 P45 engine was a V-12, water-cooled, 21-liter power plant that could develop a maximum of 650 horsepower at 3,000 rpm. In addition to the fender bolts, one of the brackets for the antipersonnel mine-launcher system can be seen at the extreme left. There were a total of five brackets for this system installed on the upper hull. *Patton Museum*

A welder fastens safety clips to a bogie wheel. The complexity of the interleaving roadwheel system is apparent here. Each axle contained three wheels, for a total of thirty-two per side. The outermost wheels, one of which is being worked on here, were left off for transport. The seams at the center of each rubber tire can be clearly seen. *Patton Museum*

Chassis number 250225 continues its journey through Henschel's Mittelfeld Werkes plant. The worker in the foreground is collecting the cables that were used to raise the hull in order to place it on the track sections seen underneath. The U-shaped shackles were threaded though the openings in the front of the hull near the final drives. *Patton Museum*

The chalked chassis number seen on the upper left of the glacis plate has been replaced with an internal build number, probably used by the paint shop or test track. Once the transport tracks were installed and the lower hull was painted, the chassis would have been taken for a test drive and then brought back to Shop 5 for final assembly. *Patton Museum*

The turret is lowered with an overhead crane in order to seat it securely in the turret ring. Paint has been applied only up to the lower edge of the hull. The remainder of the vehicle would have still been finished with red primer. At this date, Tigers were to be painted *Dunkelgelb* (dark yellow: RAL 7028). *Patton Museum*

Closer inspection of the front hull reveals the chassis number of this Tiger I, hull number 240236. Interestingly, both the headlights and the interior of the machine gun mount are painted, while the remainder of the upper hull and turret is not. This tank would later be assigned to *Panzergrenadier Division Großdeutschland*. *Patton Museum*

Tigers have now moved to another station within the factory, where they will have all the remaining external equipment installed, such as tools, tow cables, and gun-cleaning rods. Final paint has been applied at this point as well. They will shortly be turned over to their assigned crews, who received their training right at the factory. *Patton Museum*

Tiger I, hull number 250234, makes its maiden drive out of the factory in May 1943, with its new commander in the turret. The outer flaps of the front mudguards have been secured in the raised position, while the fenders and outer roadwheels are absent in preparation for rail travel. The spare-track holders on the turret will receive links from the unit workshop upon arrival there. *Patton Museum*

The crew take their places in preparation for the move to the railhead. They will be responsible for securing it for transport. The full-width battle tracks, side fenders, and additional roadwheels will be carefully stowed beneath the tank on its railcar during its journey. Some hard work is ahead for this crew. *Patton Museum*

Tiger I, chassis number 250234, became a mount of *schwere Panzerabteilung 502* in May 1943. Its next stop will be a training area in Augan, France—at the old French artillery firing range of Coëtquidan. There, the commanders and crews will acquaint themselves with their new tanks and undergo gunnery training. Ammunition, battle tracks, outer roadwheels, and spare track links will all be added upon arrival. The *502* saw combat entirely on the Eastern Front and was the very first unit to receive the Tiger I in 1942. *Patton Museum*

A view from the commander's position of a Tiger I. These are also tanks of *schwere Panzer Abteilung 502*, and Tigers are all May production examples recently obtained at the Henschel factory. To the rear of the commander, one of two hollow posts for a rain cover can be seen. Bullet cartridges and boxes are scattered on the turret roof. *Patton Museum*

Additional photos showing *schwere Panzer Abteilung 502* at the Coëtquidan range training on their new Tiger I tanks. In the background is the abandoned Château du Bois du Loup, obtained when the land was purchased by the French army before the First World War. The tank in the foreground is the mount of *Oberleutnant* Böher, with other May production tanks around it. *Patton Museum*

Oberleutnant Böher's tank moves off the road surface. This angle provides a good perspective of the tank's design and equipment at this stage of its development. It still retains many of the earlier features, such as the S-mine launchers, the *Feifel* air cleaners, and the larger shovel on the glacis plate. The armored periscope cover for the loader was introduced in May. *Patton Museum*

Tigers of the *2nd SS Panzer Grenadier Division "Das Reich"* travel along a forest track near Kirovograd, in central Ukraine, in December 1943. The forward tank is a model of post–May 1943 production. It retains the toggle bolts on either side of the MG mount (eliminated in June) yet has the loader's periscope introduced in May 1943. It is most likely a survivor of the summer Kursk battles, as indicated by the presence of the *doppel-balken* rune insignia on the left upper hull. This was introduced just prior to the battle. The tank also has numerous small hits on the glacis plate. *Bundesarchiv*

A brand-new cast commander's cupola design was introduced in production in July 1943. It was lower in profile and had a ring for an antiaircraft machine gun. The presence of *Zimmerit*, an August introduction, and the absence of the front-mounted headlight (October) demonstrate that this Tiger was produced in the late summer of 1943. It is assigned to the *schwere Panzer Abteilung 501* and is seen here during Operation *Hubertus*, a counterattack by the 256th Infantry Division on the Eastern Front in mid-March 1944. *Patton Museum*

A Tiger crew of an unknown unit replenishes the tank's ammunition on the Eastern Front. A small section of the commander's antiaircraft MG mount can be seen at the top of the turret at center left. Although it has been largely obscured by the roughly applied winter whitewash, this Tiger has a coat of factory-applied *Zimmerit* antimagnetic paste, pointing to summer 1943 production.
Patton Museum

Tiger number "301" of *schwere Panzer Abteilung 501* has become inextricably mired in mud, although the crew eventually recovered it by using timbers beneath the tracks and drove it out under its own power. This is another late-summer-production Tiger I with *Zimmerit* and the later commander's cupola.
Patton Museum

The Maybach engine of a Tiger I belonging to the *Großdeutschland Division* is removed by a Büssing NAG 4500A truck mounting a 3-ton Bilstein crane in the autumn of 1944. This is likely a vehicle that was produced post–August 1943, since it lacks the turret smoke-grenade launcher arrays eliminated in May, yet has *Zimmerit* antimagnetic coating introduced in August 1943. *Patton Museum*

This photo provides a clear view of the Bilstein 3-ton crane as it holds the Maybach engine suspended at the rear of Tiger number A31. Near the bottom of the winch housing of the crane are a large data plate and weight indicator. The German army of World War II had a well-deserved reputation for quick field repair. Many tanks that would have been otherwise written off were swiftly returned to combat. *Patton Museum*

The vehicle seen here is a rarely seen production version of the Tiger I. The tank features the later cast cupola, but only a single Bosch light mounted on the left side of the hull. It sports a full factory coating of *Zimmerit*, but the tracks do not yet have their distinctive chevrons. This puts its date of manufacture somewhere between August and September 1943. The angle of the barrel indicates that the internal gun travel lock has been engaged. This photo also shows the more forward location for the turret ventilator (directly over the gun breech), a feature introduced in July 1943. *Patton Museum*

These Tiger I tanks are loaded on flatcars for cross-country transport and provide an interesting comparison of tanks produced in March 1943 (in the foreground) and those produced during summer 1943 (to its rear). Welded over the gunsight apertures on the foreground tank's mantlet is a small plate, probably intended as a sunscreen. Both tanks are wearing their wider operational tracks rather than the narrower transport tracks. *Patton Museum*

Panzerkampfwagen VI Ausf. E (Tiger I)	
Length	8.45 m (27.7 ft.)
Width	3.70 m (12.1 ft.)
Height	2.93 m (9.6 ft.)
Weight	57 tons
Fuel capacity	540 liters (142.6 gallons)
Maximum speed	38 km/hr (23.6 mph)
Range, on road	140 km (86.8 mi.)
Range, cross country	110 km (68.2 mi.)
Crew	5
Communications	FuG 5

Armament	
Weapon, main	8.8 cm KwK 36 L/56
Weapon, coaxial	7.92 mm MG 34
Weapon, ball mounted	7.92 mm MG 34
Ammo stowage, main	93 rounds
Ammo stowage, secondary	4,800 rounds
Automotive	
Engine make	Maybach
Engine model	HL210 P45
Engine configuration	V-12, liquid cooled
Engine displacement	21.0 liters (5.5 gallons)
Engine horsepower	690 @ 3,000 rpm

This Tiger, "133" of the 1st Company, *schwere SS Panzer Abteilung 101*, was commanded by *SS-Oberscharführer* Fritz Zahner. It is seen here passing through the village of Morgny, Normandy, on June 7, 1944. The center-mounted headlight was introduced into production in October 1943, while the shovel and brackets (visible here) were eliminated in January 1944. *Patton Museum*

A classic midproduction Tiger I of the 3rd Company of *schwere Panzer Abteilung 508* is seen here along an Italian highway during the advance from Ficulle to the Anzio beachhead in February 1944. All visible features point to production in the late fall of 1943. *Patton Museum*

Another view of the *schwere Panzer Abteilung 508* Tiger I from a slightly different angle. Although this tank still has the clasps for the large glacis-mounted shovel, it appears to have been replaced with a long wrecking bar. The track-pulling cable on the left side of the hull appears to be in disarray, indicating recent use. *Bundesarchiv*

Two Tiger Is produced in fall 1943 prepare for combat in the winter of 1943–44. The distinctive cleats seen on the track faces were introduced into production at Henschel in October 1943 and were meant to improve the grip of the tracks on snow and ice. *Patton Museum*

After its arrival in Romania in 1944, this crew of the 2nd Platoon, 9th Company, 3rd Battalion, *Großdeutschland Panzer Regiment*, switches its narrow transport tracks for the wider combat tracks. The collapsed travel lock seen on the right rear hull was used in production from November 1943 until February 1944. *Patton Museum*

A *Brummbär* self-propelled assault gun eases past a disabled Tiger of the 3rd Company, *schwere Panzer Abteilung 508*, in Italy. In the background, two 18-ton half-tracks are preparing for its recovery. The center-mounted headlight marks this tank as a model produced post–October 1943. *Patton Museum*

The *schwere Panzer Abteilung 508* detrained at Ficulle, Italy, in February 1944 while en route to the Anzio-Nettuno front. The battalion then made a 125-mile road march through Rome, sidelining several Tigers to breakdowns. This is yet another post–October 1943 machine. *Bundesarchiv*

A Tiger of the 3rd Company, *schwere Panzer Abteilung 508*, rumbles through the Piazza de Venezia in Rome while en route to the Anzio-Nettuno beachheads. Like many other Tigers from this unit, the larger shovel on the glacis plate has been replaced with a wrecking bar. Two additional crewman have come along for the ride. *Bundesarchiv*

In February 1944, a Tiger I of the 1st Company, *schwere Panzer Abteilung 508*, travels toward the Allied beachhead at Anzio-Nettuno. A number of infantrymen are onboard, some wearing overcoats. The two cables are loosely arrayed on the upper hull so that they will be easily accessible in the event of a recovery under fire. *Bundesarchiv*

A general officer rides a Tiger past civilians and troops on the Eastern Front in late 1944. In this photo the turret ventilator can be seen just to the right of the main gun. This was its new location as of July 1943, concurrent with the introduction of the new commander's cupola. The turret roof was also increased in thickness from 25 mm to 40 mm at this time. *Patton Museum*

A Tiger I of *schwere SS Panzer Abteilung 101* rolls before the camera in a staged shot in the spring of 1944. The unit was heavily engaged later in Normandy. Several visible features can date the production of this tank. The external travel lock for the 88 mm gun at the right rear of the deck was introduced in November 1943 and discontinued in February 1944. The presence of the older loader's hatch (with the longer hinges) points to an earlier date, since is was officially discontinued in March. Quantities remained in production until exhausted. *Patton Museum*

This crewman is part of a major overhaul of a Tiger I. He has begun the process of removing the air cleaners on the top of the engine. To his left is the automatic fire extinguisher bottle, which could hold 3 liters of chemical flame retardant. The fuel filler flange to the right of his head is of an unusual round shape. This area is typically surrounded by a squared flange. *Patton Museum*

Tiger tactical number "217" of *schwere Panzer Abteilung 502* negotiates a small depression on the Eastern Front in the spring of 1944. This vehicle is a post–February 1944 production, as noted by its redesigned front side-hull extensions. They were lengthened and notched to allow the C-tow hooks to swivel freely. The older design was seen until at least chassis number 250829. *Patton Museum*

A knocked-out Tiger of *schwere SS Panzer Abteilung 101*, of post–February 1944 production, sits at the intersection of Rue Jeanne Bacon and Rue Saint-Emile Sanson in Villers-Bocage on June 13, 1944. In addition to the other more obvious damage, fire has destroyed the torsion bars inside the tank, causing it to lower closer to the ground. *Bundesarchiv*

Significant changes were made in the appearance of the Tiger toward the end of its production run. In February 1944, at chassis number 250822, new all-steel roadwheels were introduced. Other notable modifications seen on this *schwere SS Panzer Abteilung 101* Tiger are the new 15 mm loader's hatch (March 1943), the wider loader's periscope cover (July 1943), and the elimination of the large glacis-mounted shovel (January 1944). *Patton Museum*

Tiger tactical number "232" was commanded by *SS-Unterscharführer* Kurt Kleber. Officially, Tigers were not allowed to be used as tow vehicles except in extraordinary circumstances. This appears to be one of those instances, due to the very real threat of Allied fighter-bombers. These photos were taken the day after the Battle of Villers-Bocage. *Bundesarchiv*

Tiger tactical number "300" of the *schwere Panzer Abteilung 505* is passed by a *SdKfz 7/1*, mounting quad 20 mm automatic cannons in an open turret on a modified 8-ton half-track. Other photos of this Tiger show that it is equipped with steel-tired roadwheels. In spite of its late date of manufacture, it still retains the earlier loader's hatch. *Patton Museum*

This Tiger I, participating in a demonstration in Poland, exhibits many late-production features, the simpler loader's hatch and revised tow shackles being prominent. Another late-production feature is the monocular gunsight in the turret. The single, rather than double, aperture in the mantlet illustrates this. This feature was introduced in April 1944, somewhere around chassis number 250990. *Bundesarchiv*

By the style of its turret numbers, this Tiger I of *schwere SS Panzer Abteilung 101* appears to be a replacement vehicle. The unit was constantly engaged in combat throughout the summer of 1944. In profile, the curved side-hull plate above the front tow shackle is more apparent here. Like most other tanks of this unit, it features a unit-made bar across the front hull for the stowage of spare track links. *Bundesarchiv*

Tiger I, tactical number "131," chassis number 250122, soon after its arrival in October 1943 at the School of Tank Technology, where it would undergo a thorough evaluation. Its capture had caused quite a sensation in Allied circles, and prior to its arrival in England the tank had been on display in Tunis, undergoing inspection there by a large group of officials including King George VI and Winston Churchill. *Patton Museum*

Other useful components traveling back to the United Kingdom from Tunisia were a set of *Verladekette* transport tracks. Here, the outer roadwheels have been removed and the narrower tracks installed. The side fender panels have also been removed, and their square bolts are clearly seen here. Note how the front and rear fender panels folded back to match the reduced width of the tank in this configuration. The engine of Tiger "131" was also extensively tested and later used as a cutaway model at the school. *Patton Museum*

Given the important nature of its presence in Tunis, it was vital that the vehicle present the best possible impression. With proper military precision in preparation for its viewing by the king and the prime minister, the Tiger was given a fresh coat of paint. This obliterated any trace of the original camouflage. The badge of the British First Army was painted on the front glacis plate and on the rear fender. *Patton Museum*

In addition to its fresh paint job, the tank was also repaired using components of other captured Tigers, most notably the replacement of the smoke launcher on the left-hand side of the top of the turret, sheared away in action the previous April. Battle damage is evident on the turret stowage box and the exhaust shield. The Tiger I was eventually transferred to the Tank Museum by the British Ministry of Supply on September 25, 1951. *Patton Museum*

At the time of this writing, this is the world's only fully operational Tiger I tank. It is, perhaps, the crown jewel of the extensive collection held at the Tank Museum at Bovington Camp in Dorset, England. At least once per year, the tank is run through its paces at an outdoor event. *Massimo Foti*

Although Tiger "131" has been mechanically restored, the museum staff has been careful to retain its original form. It has been located in Dorset since October 1943, when it was sent to the School of Tank Technology for evaluation. *Massimo Foti*

The Bovington Tiger is serial number 250122, and Henschel completed it in February 1943. It is formerly a mount of the 3rd Platoon, 1st Company, *schwere Panzer Abteilung 504*. It arrived in Tunisia sometime between March 22 and April 16, 1943. *Massimo Foti*

Tiger "131" on display inside the Tank Museum. The British unit responsible for its capture was the 48th Royal Tank Regiment, A Squadron, 4th Troop. This occurred on April 21, 1943, after an engagement at Djebel Djaffa, Tunisia. *Massimo Foti*

Carefully preserved is the shrapnel damage incurred during its last engagement. Perforations are visible to the sheet-metal exhaust covers, as well as to the right *Feifel* air-cleaning canister. *Massimo Foti*

The left-hand side of the rear plate reveals the other *Feifel* air-cleaning canister, the track toolbox below it, and the folding rear fender flap. Pulling the square lever released the outer panel, allowing it to be folded upward. *Massimo Foti*

An overall view of the rear engine deck. This shot illustrates the complete air-cleaning system. Known as *Feifel* after its manufacturer, it was a two-stage filtering system for engine air intake in dusty conditions. *Massimo Foti*

The system was first installed on vehicles bound for Tunisia. The intake tubes are seen to the inside here. They fed air into the bottom of each filter canister. The outer tubes fed clean air into the engine compartment. *Massimo Foti*

A view of the turret from the rear, showing the turret stowage bin. It was constructed of thin sheet metal, and its components were fastened with small rivets. Two lockable doors were located on either side. The box was notched in the center to accommodate the center turret-lifting lug. *Massimo Foti*

An overall view of the turret roof. To the rear of the photo is the commander's cupola. In the right foreground is the loader's hatch. To the left is the turret ventilator housing. A detachable cover for deepwater fording is often seen installed on the housing. This was discarded on later model Tigers. *Massimo Foti*

The commander's cupola. A sliding lever with a sprung base controlled the hatch. The square metal post at the rear acted as a hatch stop. The horizontal slits corresponded to internally mounted glass blocks. The small holes around its circumference drained water away from the inner lip. The two short, vertical tubes were used to mount a small rain shield. *Massimo Foti*

This view of the front right-hand corner of the turret reveals the thick, robust nature of its armored construction. To the extreme left is a vision slit, while forward and above that is the smoke launcher array. At center is the right-hand pivot point for the gun mantlet. This also served as one of three points for lifting the turret. The aperture for the coaxial MG 34 is seen to the right. *Massimo Foti*

On the left side of the turret, some additional original damage can be seen. A round from a Churchill tank caused the gouge on the turret-lifting lug. This also sheared off the topmost tube of the smoke-grenade launcher. This was later replaced with a part from another Tiger I. The binocular gunsight aperture is visible to the extreme left. *Massimo Foti*

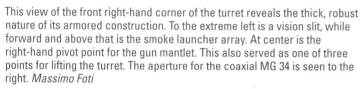

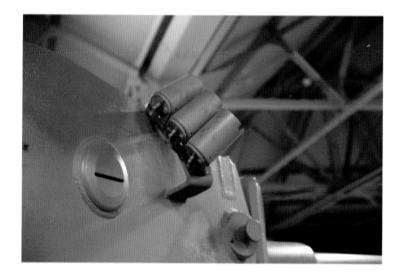

This is the base of the smoke launcher array. An electrical lead exited the turret roof and was connected to three insulators on the bottom of each tube. Small retaining chains kept the insulators from falling away in the event the wires were severed. When all six tubes were fired, an effective smoke screen could be created. The Germans referred to the smoke grenades as *Schelinebelkerze* (NbK-39). *Massimo Foti*

Additional tool stowage could be found on the top of the hull between the driver's and radio operator's hatches. To the front of the driver's hatch is stowed a sledgehammer, while behind and to the left is a smaller shovel and an ax. The hull ventilator cover is to left center, and beyond that at the extreme left is the jack block. *Massimo Foti*

This higher view shows the long weld seam that crosses the width of the turret roof. The indentations at the center are screwheads that secure the internal travel lock for the main gun. The electrical lead for the smoke-grenade launcher is visible at the lower right. *Massimo Foti*

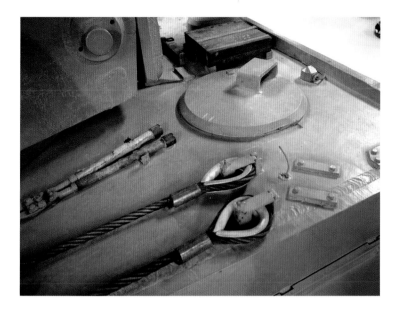

Hinged cable clasps for the 8.2 m (26.9 ft.) tow cables were located on the top of the hull; two sets on each side. Each clasp is fastened by means of a threaded post and wing nut. The cables here are not original. Forward of the clasps is one of four bases for mounting S-mine antipersonnel grenades. The electrical lead for the tube can also be seen. *Massimo Foti*

A closer view of the armored driver's visor. The center portion was raised or lowered by means of a small-wheeled knob inside. A large armored glass block 70 mm thick covered the opening in front of the driver. The two small indentations above the visor were originally intended as apertures for a driver's periscope but were deleted in February 1943 production. *Massimo Foti*

A large shovel was stowed on the forward portion of the glacis plate. This was a unique feature of the Tiger I. The ball mount for the hull MG 34 is seen behind the shovel. On either side are threaded and hinged posts for the mounting of a deepwater-fording cover. The driver's visor is to the far right. *Massimo Foti*

Looking down the left-hand side from the front, another tow cable array can be seen. A gun-cleaning rod, broken down into three threaded sections, was stowed on brackets between the cable. To the left of the cable is a panel for sealing the engine air intake during fording. A base for an S-mine launcher is seen in the center foreground, while in the extreme foreground, a light base and its electrical lead are also visible. *Massimo Foti*

A somewhat menacing frontal view of the Tiger I. Although the tank has been repainted several times, the museum staff has strived to make the current scheme as close as possible to the original. The spare track holder on the front hull and the step are unit-made additions. *Massimo Foti*

The thinner cable mounted along the left side was used for the installation and removal of transportation tracks. The original was 15 m long and was held in place by small, hinged clamps similar in design to those used on the top of the hull. The tactical insignia accurately reflects a tank of the 1st Company. *Massimo Foti*

The front fenders, like the rear ones, could be folded up by actuating the square-shaped lever in the middle. This action reduced their width equal to that of the hull. With the side fender panels removed and narrow transportation tracks installed, the Tiger was fit for rail travel throughout Europe. *Massimo Foti*

The Tiger I used a series of interleaved roadwheels in order to suspend its immense weight. The roadwheel sets were attached to eight torsion bars on each side. Three roadwheels were mounted on each axle. The outermost roadwheels, one of which is seen here, were removable for rail travel. Once again, original shrapnel damage can be seen on the wheel. *Massimo Foti*

This late-model Tiger I is located at the French Tank Museum, known as the Musée des Blindés, in the town of Saumur in the Loire valley. It is chassis number 251114 and is one of the last hundred or so to be manufactured, leaving the factory in May 1944. It originally had the tactical number "114" on its turret when it was part of the 1st Company of the *SS Panzer Abteilung 102. Massimo Foti*

The muzzle brake is offset at an angle due to the loosening of the setscrew seen at the lower right. Normally, this screw would have faced directly up. *Massimo Foti*

The characteristic curved profile of the front tow shackle. This vehicle has a very thoroughly applied coating of *Zimmerit* antimagnetic paste added after its arrival at the museum. The fenders are not original to the tank. *Massimo Foti*

The massive mantlet of the Tiger I. This shot illustrates another characteristic feature of late-production Tiger Is: the monocular gunsight aperture. *Massimo Foti*

The drive sprocket of the Tiger had a substantial cast base that mounted a machined outer segment. The large, star-shaped fixture on the sprocket face was added to help secure the bolts against vibration. This feature entered production at chassis 251205 and was added to this vehicle after its manufacture. *Massimo Foti*

In order to reduce the amount of mud and debris that built up on the idler wheel, a smaller 600 mm part replaced the earlier 700 mm part late in production. *Massimo Foti*

The glacis plate of the Tiger I was 120 mm thick. The single front light and hanger are features introduced in October 1943. The hooks seen at the left and right of the glacis plate are for hanging spare track sections.
Massimo Foti

This Tiger I was abandoned by its crew in late August 1944 and captured by the French near Cauville in Normandy. Because it remained in operational condition, the French it put it back into service against its former owners. It would serve with the *6eme Regiment de Cuirassiers* until the end of the war.
Massimo Foti

This small armored plate could be removed to adjust the idler wheel arm, and there is a duplicate on the right side. The museum has added replacement fender sections to the rear hull. The remnants of a marker light are visible at the lower left. *Massimo Foti*

The French made some modifications to the Tiger I during its service life, including welding short sections of curved pipe on the top of the exhaust stack, replacing the original hinged flaps. Flame could occasionally shoot from the vertical stacks, and these pipes helped direct it to the rear. *Massimo Foti*

A rhomboid-shaped plate was provided to facilitate use of a manual starting mechanism. It is normally stowed on posts between the exhaust stacks, near the top of the hull. Just below the plate is a tow pintle. *Massimo Foti*

The overall layout of the rear hull is evident here. The two large posts for stowing the starter guide can be seen clearly. Stowage for a 20-ton jack was provided on the right side of the hull, and the posts to the extreme left are for the stowage of a large C-shaped towing hook. *Massimo Foti*

The Saumur Tiger I mounts the less typical 520 mm transport track, as opposed to the required 725 mm battle track. It's not clear if this was a wartime fitting, or if these tracks were mounted during testing after the war. *Massimo Foti*

Replacing the Tiger I was the better-armed and better-armored Tiger II. This vehicle too was designed by Henschel. During the course of production, two styles of turrets were used. Three prototypes and the initial forty-seven production vehicles had turrets designed by Henschel that were intended for Porsche's aborted Tiger program, the VK 45.02 (P). As a result, for decades these vehicles have somewhat erroneously been known as "Porsche turret" Tiger IIs.

Subsequent vehicles were built with a turret specially engineered for the Tiger II, which corrected the shot trap presented by the expedient installation of the VK 45.02 (P) turrets. Regardless of turret design, mounted on it was a powerful 8.8 cm L/71 KwK 43 cannon. This gun, derived from the 88 mm FlaK 41, was mandated for the Tiger II by Hitler himself.

While the name would imply that the Tiger II was a follow-on to the Tiger Tank *Ausführung E*, in reality the only component of consequence brought over from the earlier design was the transmission, and that was modified.

Production of the Tiger II began in January 1944. These vehicles, being even more sophisticated than the Tiger I, were a challenge to produce and consumed large resources. Accordingly, even though it remained in production through March 1945, only 474 were completed. Despite the low production numbers, their virtual handmade nature meant that there were numerous variations. In addition to the previously mentioned turret change, other variances had to do with the deletion of the telescoping snorkel used for fording.

In April 1944, changes were made near the two shackles on the front and rear hull extensions so as to allow the use of "C" hooks. At about the same time, a four-segment turret ring guard was added, requiring a change in the screens on the engine deck. A notch in the glacis near the radio operator's periscope was introduced at this time as well.

Also, the binocular T.Z.F. 9b/1 gunner's sight was replaced with the monocular T.Z.F 9d sight, and as a result the left sight hole in the turret face was plugged.

Beginning in April 1944, an easier-to-manufacture two-piece gun barrel was introduced, replacing the earlier one-piece, or monoblock, gun tube.

A new track design was introduced in May 1944. While more rigid than the older Gg 24/800/300, and thus having a higher rolling resistance, the new track was also less likely to work its way off the drive sprocket. The new track, the Gg 26/800/300, required a new drive sprocket that had only nine teeth, as compared to the eighteen-tooth sprocket used previously.

Bolted rather than welded assembly began to be used to mount the commander's cupola in August 1944.

The weld seam, a prominent feature on earlier models, obviously is absent from the tanks with the cupola bolted in place. Also in August, the Tiger IIs began to leave the factory in a production-applied three-color camouflage scheme. That lasted only about a month before material shortages and the urgency of production brought about the vehicles being shipped painted only in their red-oxide primer, to which patches of dark yellow, red brown, and olive green could be added.

During October 1944, installation of the 20-ton jack and the corresponding mounting brackets ceased.

Relatively few changes occurred until January 1945, when the Henschel assembly plant began to receive armor components prepainted in RAL 6003 olive green. After assembly, RAL 8017 red-brown and RAL 7028 were sprayed onto the vehicles in a hard-edge camouflage scheme.

The last major change came in March 1945, just before US troops captured the Henschel factory. A new track, the Kgs 73/800/152 single-link track, was introduced. This required once again utilizing an eighteen-tooth drive sprocket. Very few tanks were produced with this track, due to the Allies taking Kassel, home of the Tiger plant.

This Tiger II exhibits all the features of a very early-production tank, most notably the turret created for the Porsche Tiger II prototype. It is probably one of four machines from February–March production to be retained by the Germans for testing and training. The spare track links mounted on the turret roof are of interest. *Patton Museum*

Panzerkampfwagen VI Ausf. B (Tiger II)	
Length	10.30 m (33.8 ft.)
Width	3.76 m (12.3 ft.)
Height	3.08 m (10.1 ft.)
Weight	68 tons
Fuel capacity	860 liters (227.0 gallons)
Maximum speed	35 km/hr (21.7 mph)
Range, on road	170 km (105.4 mi.)
Range, cross country	120 km (74.4)
Crew	5
Communications	FuG 5

Armament	
Weapon, main	8.8 cm KwK 43 L/71
Weapon, coaxial	7.92 mm MG 34
Weapon, ball mounted	7.92 mm MG 34
Ammo stowage, main	86 rounds (80 rounds with "Porsche" turret)
Ammo stowage, secondary	5,850 rounds

Automotive	
Engine make	Maybach
Engine model	HL230 P30
Engine configuration	V-12, liquid cooled
Engine displacement	23 liters (6.1 gallons)
Engine horsepower	700 @ 3,000 rpm

The same tank as seen in the previous photo. Seen here to good advantage are the openings for the binocular TZF 9b/1 gunner's sight on the left side of the turret. In April, one of the openings was welded over to accommodate a monocular sight. Also visible at the lower left are the troublesome Gg 24/800/300 multipart tracks. These were eliminated in production in May 1944. *Patton Museum*

One of the original four Tiger IIs still remaining at the German testing facilities at Haustenbeck at the war's end. This is thought to be either chassis number 280009 or 280012. It had been fitted with the late-war Kgs 73/800/152 single-link cross-country tracks. These were later refitted to the V2 prototype by the British. The main gun was spiked by the facility's staff. *Patton Museum*

The very first unit on the Western Front to receive the Tiger II was the *schwere Panzer Abteilung 503.* These were likely from a production block that exited the Henschel facility in April and May 1944. This and the next two photos show the new tanks undergoing gunnery training at the *Wehrmacht* training center close to the village of Mailly-le-Camp in northern France. This was a large complex originally built for the French army in 1902.
Patton Museum

Several of the Tiger IIs in these photos still mount the earlier, simplified version of the KwK 43 L/71 barrel. A sectional tube with a stepped-sleeve construction was introduced in mid-April. The vehicle in the foreground has not yet mounted its fender panels. In order to keep the new 8.8 cm gun as clean as possible, the crew has assembled the full gun-cleaning rod and has placed it on the right-hand track run for easy access.
Patton Museum

Gunnery training for the 3rd Company of *schwere Panzer Abteilung 503* continues. Tanks that were not specifically engaging their target were required to raise their barrels. This allowed observers to ascertain who was hitting their marks and when. The crew of Tiger "334" has also wisely kept their assembled gun-cleaning rod ready. It can be seen threaded through the right-hand brackets.
Patton Museum

Tiger IIs of the 1st Company *schwere Panzer Abteilung 503* laager in the woods in early July 1944, where they were responding to the British beachheads north of Caen. The tank in the foreground has the later sectional gun barrel tube with a stepped sleeve. Both visible Tiger IIs are prepared for quick recovery in combat with C-hooks and tow cables attached.
Patton Museum

A tank of the 3rd Company rumbles into the assembly area. The *schwere Panzer Abteilung 503* was probably up to full strength as it prepared to engage the Allied armies landing in France. It normally would have fielded forty-five Tigers within three companies. Each company had three platoons of four Tigers. In addition, two command tanks were assigned to each company, and three were issued to the battalion command. *National Archives*

The Tank Museum at Bovington holds one of the three original prototype Tiger IIs. It had been completed in January 1944 and then diverted from Henschel for trials at a testing area in Haustenbeck, Germany. It was there that the British captured it at the end of the war. *Massimo Foti*

When captured, the Tiger II had been mounting the early, multipart Gg 24/800/300 tracks. These were later replaced with a set of Kgs 73/800/152 single-link cross-country tracks obtained from a second Tiger II at Haustenbeck. These tracks were a recent innovation at the time, having been put into production only in March 1945. *Massimo Foti*

The first fifty tanks produced, including the prototype, mounted what became known as the Porsche turret. This turret was actually designed by Krupp for use on the Porsche VK 45.02 (P), which was never produced. A residual deficiency of its use was the large shot trap, seen here in profile. *Massimo Foti*

The Tiger II drive sprocket was similar to that of the Tiger I, in that it was a combination of cast and machined parts. The original eighteen-tooth sprocket ring was replaced by a nine-tooth ring in May 1944, in conjunction with a new track design. Oddly, the eighteen-tooth design was reintroduced in March 1945 with the new Kgs 73/800/152 single-link tracks. *Massimo Foti*

Like the Tiger I, the Tiger II used torsion bars and interleaved roadwheels. These metal tired wheels contained inner rubber bushings. Although similar in design to those used on the Tiger I, they were not the same diameter and therefore not interchangeable. *Massimo Foti*

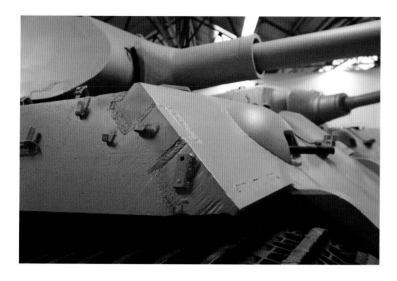

The large interlocking lugs and weld beads of the front 150 mm armor plate are clearly seen here. The upper side armor plates were 80 mm thick. To the right is the ball mount for the hull-mounted MG 34 with its armored barrel. *Massimo Foti*

Details of the interlocking armor plates on the early turret. The forming of this 100 mm front plate was considered expensive and time-consuming. The later design was much simpler. *Massimo Foti*

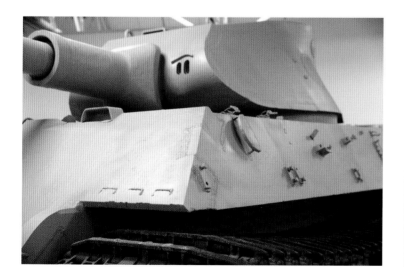

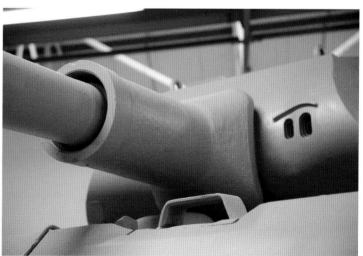

The upper-left hull corner. At the time of its capture, this Tiger II mounted flat front fenders very similar to those used on the Tiger I. Remnants of their welded attachments points are still visible. Note how the front armored plate is chamfered to aid in the use of the hull-mounted periscope. *Massimo Foti*

The large, curved gun mount of the first fifty tanks was designed to match the rounded profile of the mantlet, but in doing so exacerbated the major deficiency of its design: rounds striking this area were directed downward into the thinner top hull armor. *Massimo Foti*

The rectangular hardware mounted to the side of the hull was used to attach lightly armored side skirts. These were meant to protect the area just above the tracks. Other hardware present was used to attach the tow cables, tools, and gun-cleaning rods. *Massimo Foti*

Another troublesome production feature was forming the bow on the left side of the turret for the commander's hatch. On the first sixteen turrets, a large shell ejection mount had been mounted, as well as a pistol port for the commander. Their openings and hinge mounts were welded over at the factory. *Massimo Foti*

The overall design of the Tiger II owed more to the Panther than that of the earlier Tiger I. This is due to the requirement that it share common parts with the proposed Panther II design. Although the Panther II never entered production, the family resemblance remained. The exhaust is fitted with a modified pipe that Henschel used to test exhaust pressure. *Massimo Foti*

A large, bolted panel was designed for the rear of the turret. It was intended to be removable in order to replace the main gun via the rear opening. The panel and hatch are missing on the Bovington vehicle and have been replaced with a wooden panel. *Massimo Foti*

The turret roof on this example was 15 mm thick, as was the loader's hatch. The turret ventilator is visible at the center. It contained flanges to mount a waterproof cover used in deepwater fording. The commander's hatch is missing on the Bovington vehicle, lost during postwar testing. *Massimo Foti*

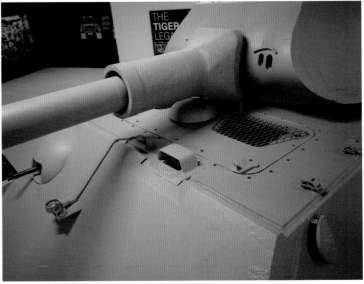

A closer view of the turret roof. A large ventilator assembly is located at top center, while just behind it is a more practical hinged shell ejection port. A lifting ring is located to the rear. Additional details of the interlocking armor plates are in evidence. *Massimo Foti*

The Bovington vehicle is also missing both the driver's and radio operator's hatches. Again, due to its similarity with the Panther design, the large panel that contained the hatches could be removed in order to service the transmission. The empty clasps at the far right were used to stow a sledgehammer. *Massimo Foti*

Schwere Panzer Abteilung 503 continued to receive new Tiger II tanks to replace their early losses, and this brand-new tank is just receiving its camouflage paint job. The Tiger II seen here and in the next three photos is probably among the first to mount the new Series turret, which entered production at chassis number 280048 in June. The absence of the side skirts provides a useful perspective of the suspension system of the Tiger B. *Patton Museum*

An excellent profile of the Series turret. Its new design solved the many production problems of the Porsche prototype turret, not the least among them the seriously complicated forging procedures involving its curved surfaces. The bell-shaped gun base was also easier to produce and was more practical from a ballistic standpoint. The crewman in the foreground is guiding the travel of the compressed air hose to keep it from fouling on the tank's external equipment. *Patton Museum*

The turret has been rotated almost 90 degrees in order to maximize the amount of hull available to receive paint. The forward corners of the production turret were chamfered to allow it to clear the driver's and radio operator's hatches. The 180 mm flat front face of the turret and the bell-shaped gun base are also evident here. The crewman on the top of the turret is preparing the new periscopes for installation. *Patton Museum*

A good close-up of the left-hand side of the hull. To the extreme left is the stowed shovel, while directly in front of the crewman is one of two 32 mm thick tow cables. The attachment bolts for the side skirts can be discerned along the edge of the hull, and a wrecking bar is seen in the background. This bar was normally stowed on the left side of the hull, just behind and above the tow cable.
Patton Museum

The *schwere Panzer Abteilung 503* was largely destroyed in the summer battles for northern France. Only two Tiger II tanks made it back to Germany after the retreat. The unit was completely refitted in early September 1944 and sent to the Eastern Front, where it was to spend the remainder of the war. This and the following four photos show the unit as it was used in response to the Hungarian officers' coup on October 15, 1944. *Patton Museum*

The *schwere Panzer Abteilung 503* had already been fighting in eastern Hungary in response to the Soviet fall offensive known as the Battle of Debrecen, when it was ordered into Budapest. This Tiger II of the 2nd Company is a classic example of summer 1944 production, with its full complement of stowage, fenders, and factory-applied coat of *Zimmerit* antimagnetic paste. The frame for the commander's machine gun can be seen behind the loader's head. *Patton Museum*

The same vehicle inches forward in the October morning fog. Although the commander appears in his combat position, the presence of a civilian working on his car indicates that this action has been contrived for the cameraman. Tiger II tactical number "233" is missing the left-rear fender panel, as well as its C-hook towing clevises. These latter items were typically stowed on the left-rear hull plate. Liquid containers are seen strewn on the engine deck. *Patton Museum*

Tiger II tactical number "234" strikes a menacing pose in Budapest's castle district on October 15, 1944, as both German and Hungarian troops mill around. This area appears to have seen heavy fighting already. This tank appears be stopped, since neither the commander nor loader appear in the turret. Barely visible on the top of the bell-shaped gun mantlet is one of three mounts for poison-gas-detection panels. The other two were located on the rear of the turret. *Patton Museum*

The double-zero tactical number of this Tiger II indicates that it is one of three tanks assigned to the *schwere Panzer Abteilung 503*'s battalion command section. The tank is being used to destroy a street barricade and has attracted a fair amount of attention. The angle of the hull as it passes over the barrier provides an excellent look at the rear hull stowage, all of which is in place. A couple of unique features are apparent, such as the commander's MG frame stowed on the rear turret hatch and the spare track link mounted between the exhausts. *Patton Museum*

This Tiger II, chassis number 280093, was produced in July 1944 and is seen here while on display at the Tank Museum in Bovington. It had been part of the headquarters company of the *schwere SS Panzer Abteilung 101*. It was abandoned by its crew at the end of August 1944 at Aux Marais, a community on the outskirts of Beauvais, France, near the Seine River. *Massimo Foti*

This vehicle mounts the more practical production turret, with its distinctive flat front. This design eliminated all the complicated forging procedures inherent in the earlier design. The *Zimmerit* antimagnetic paste is very well preserved on this example. *Massimo Foti*

Like the Tiger I had before it, the Tiger II also introduced a modified tow shackle to improve the travel of its related hardware. This was seen after April 1944 production and followed a similar introduction on the Tiger I production line in February. Remnants of the fender hardware are seen on the hull corner.
Massimo Foti

The single front-mounted Bosch headlight is seen here with the machine gun ball mount behind it. The barrel of the protruding machine gun was lightly armored to prevent its damage by shrapnel.
Massimo Foti

The driver's hatch on this example is frozen in a slightly raised position. Also seen here is the milled chamfer for the driver's periscope—a shared trait with earlier hulls. Note how the turret is milled at its corner to clear the hull components. *Massimo Foti*

Three sections of threaded wooden rod were mounted within brackets on each side of the hull. These were used to create a single, long cleaning rod for maintaining the substantial length of the KwK 43 main gun. *Massimo Foti*

Steel hangers were welded onto each side of the turret in order to mount spare track links. These were mounted horizontally, in comparison to the vertical mounts on the Tiger I, in order to make it easier for the crew to lift them on and off. *Massimo Foti*

Just to the rear of the stowage for the gun-cleaning rod, a single-piece crank arm was stowed for manual turnover of the engine. The double-hole flanges of the Tiger II's fender panels can be clearly seen here. *Massimo Foti*

An overall view of the left side. Also like the Tiger I, the Tiger II carried two 8.2 m tow cables. Each was attached via a series of brackets. On the Tiger I, these cables were stowed on the top of the hull.
Massimo Foti

This view of the Tiger II previously held at Fort Knox, Kentucky, reveals several details of the rear hull. Seen at the left are brackets for the stowage of the two large C-hooks used for recovery operations. A bracket for a 20-ton jack was mounted across the bottom of the rear hull. *Don Moriarty*

The rear engine deck. Antigrenade screens can be seen on the air intakes on the far side of the deck. The engine access door is tucked under the rear of the turret, and the turret would have to be rotated to 90 degrees in order to open it. *Massimo Foti*

On the right side of the Fort Knox Tiger II, the brackets for the mounting of a wooden jack block can be seen near the top of the rear hull. The right-side armored exhaust cover had a small bracket on the lower portion to guide the engine start crank. *Don Moriarty*

Visible here are the fire extinguisher, antenna base, and one of two large antigrenade screens located beneath the turret bustle (*lower right*). One of the fuel vent lines is also visible at the upper left. *Massimo Foti*

The rear turret hatch served not only as a means for crew egress, but also as a way to change the barrel on the main gun. The hatch contained a handle (broken off here) and a large pistol port. Armored hinge covers normally covered the torsion bars on either side, but they are also missing here. *Massimo Foti*

An overall view of the massive turret of the Tiger II. The side armor of the turret was 80 mm thick at 21 degrees, while the front face was 180 mm thick at 10 degrees. The turret roof contained 40 mm armor plate. The loops between the track hangers could be threaded with a track pin. *Massimo Foti*

The cupola of the Tiger II was similar in design to that of the late-model Tiger I. It contained a large armored ring around its circumference for a frame that mounted an antiaircraft MG 34 or MG 42. The two short, hollow, vertical rods were for mounting a rain cover. *Don Moriarty*

On the right-side hull front, near the radio operator's hatch, an ax was stowed. The smaller cable mounted on the right hull side was 14 mm thick and 15 m (49 ft.) long. Like on the Tiger I, it was used to assist the changing of the narrower transport tracks. *Massimo Foti*

The turret roof layout had the commander's hatch on the left with the loader's hatch on the right. An armored cover for the loader's periscope was directly in front of the loader's hatch. The small vane sight seen at the right corresponded to two welded rods on the front of the cupola. *Massimo Foti*

A closer view of the radio operator's hatch, illustrating its proximity to the main gun. The large, bell-shaped gun base was a single cast piece and very atypical for German wartime production. Interestingly, the main gun was not centered in the turret; it was slightly offset to the right to make room for the gunner's sight. *Massimo Foti*

This Tiger II was not always on display in Bovington. After its recovery by Royal Engineers in January 1945, it was brought back to the United Kingdom, where it was kept at the Fighting Vehicle Proving Establishment in Chertsey. Later, it was on private display at the Royal Military College at Shrivenham before being sent to the Tank Museum in 2006. *Massimo Foti*

Due to the change in track links in May 1944, the original eighteen-tooth-drive sprocket rings were modified to have only nine teeth. This was accomplished by cutting off every other drive tooth and grinding the area smooth, a procedure still evident on this example. *Don Moriarty*

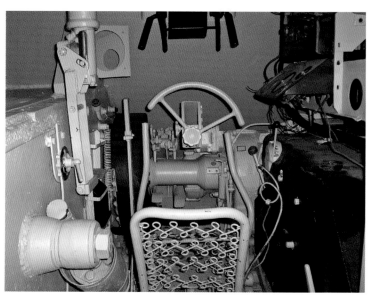

The driver's station on the Tiger II. He operated the tank via a Maybach OLVAR water-cooled EG 40 12 16 B gearbox, which provided him with eight forward and four reverse speeds. Braking was either by lever or pedal. The lever at the left could be locked for emergency extra steering. *Don Moriarty*

The second, fourth, sixth, and eighth roadwheel on either side of the Tiger II had this elongated hub. The first, third, fifth, seventh, and ninth wheels used a flush-mounted deign. *Don Moriarty*

The breech of the L/71 KwK 43 8.8 cm main gun. The tubing present was part of a compressed-air system used to evacuate fumes made by the combustion of the rounds. The shield on the left protected the turret's occupants from the recoil action. *Don Moriarty*

A small frame and roller were installed on the bottom of the rear turret bustle in order to facilitate the removal of the main gun. The interior of the commander's cupola is visible at the top of the photo. *Don Moriarty*

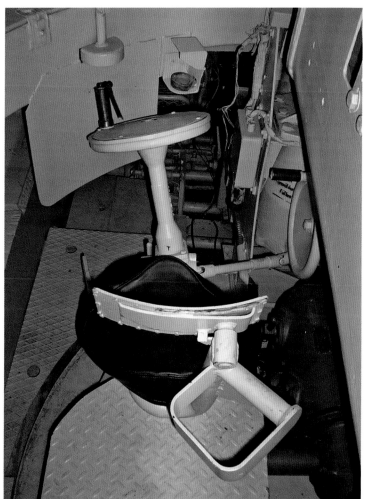

This is the gunner's position of the Tiger II. Visible to the right of the seat cushion is the elevation hand wheel. While the vehicle had power turret traverse, this required that the engine be running. To traverse the turret without the engine running, or in the event of a hydraulic system failure, the gunner used the hand wheel that is at center, whose shaft is oriented almost vertically. However, this was laborious, as a full 360-degree rotation of the turret required 700 turns of the hand wheel. *Don Moriarty*

Stowage for twelve rounds of main-gun ammunition was available on either side of the rear turret. A total of eighty-six rounds were carried throughout the vehicle. Types consisted of PzGr 39/43 (armor piercing, tungsten core), PzGr 40/43 (armor piercing, tungsten core), SprGr 43 (high explosive), and HlGr 39 (hollow charge). *Don Moriarty*

The world's only operational Tiger II tank is located at the French Tank Museum, Musée des Blindés, in the town of Saumur in the Loire Valley. It is chassis number 280112 (produced in July 1944) and was formerly a tank of the *SS Panzer Abteilung 102*. Because of the large number of Tiger IIs abandoned in France, some of its history is speculative. It is likely that this was one of several Tiger IIs abandoned on August 23, 1944, at Brueil-en-Vexin. *Massimo Foti*

Most, if not all, of the exterior equipment is missing from this example. The tank was probably salvaged by the French Army in September 1944, and then tested at the AMX factory at Satory for several years. Loose items would have been quickly lost in the months following its abandonment. A smaller 15-ton jack has been put in place by the museum staff. *Massimo Foti*

In this close-up of the turret, the interior of the loader's hatch can be seen. The hand wheel actuated the four arms arranged in an x-shape in order to secure the latch. One of the track hanger hooks has been bent down—from an impact that must have been substantial in order to damage this heavy steel part. Like other surviving Tiger IIs, this example is missing the armored guards for the torsion arms for the rear hatch. *Massimo Foti*

Also added at some point during its stay at the museum are the two cables on the hull sides. These are of a lighter gauge than the originals and would not be used to recover the Tiger II. The starter crank seen on the left side is also a modern replacement. This item is used on a regular basis, as the conventional starting system of this tank has long ceased to function. The *Zimmerit* coating is original and is in excellent condition. *Massimo Foti*

The Tiger II represented the pinnacle of Nazi Germany's production tank development. Heavily armored, mounting a potent 88 mm cannon, and benefiting from sloping armor, the tank was poised to rule the battlefield. However, limited production capacity, heavy fuel consumption, and a design that pushed the limits of manufacturing capability meant that only 492 would be built, and today only one preserved example remains operational. *Massimo Foti*